TABLE OF CONTENTS

Eastern
Hemisphere

Western
Hemisphere

Water covers 70 percent of the Earth's surface.
During river floods (above), water covers
the surrounding land. Ocean waves (below) can
cause flooding of coastal areas.

A New True Book

FLOODS

By Arlene Erlbach

Acknowledgment
David Hunter, P.E. Project Manager, Programs/Project Management,
Division of U.S. Army Corps of Engineers, Chicago District

CHILDRENS PRESS®

CHICAGO

A truck is trapped by floodwaters
on a Chicago expressway.

Dedicated to the Saturday Critique Group

PHOTO CREDITS
The Bettmann Archive—14, 34 (top right)
© Cameramann International, Ltd.—2, 29
(left), 36 (2 photos), 38
H. Armstrong Roberts—© D. Carriere, 4
(bottom)
Photri—12, 31 (left), 33 (right); © James
Kirby, 9; © H. Hungerford, 20
Reuters/Bettmann—10, 26 (right), 28
Root Resources—© Garry D. McMichael,
Cover, 7, (left), 44-45; © Steve Crook, 26
(left), 43
© Scott T. Smith—23 (left)
SuperStock International, Inc.—4
Tony Stone Images—© Jerald P. Fish, 41
UPI/Bettmann—14 (inset), 24 (2 photos), 34
(left and bottom right)
Valan—© Harold V. Green, 6; © Richard
Nowitz, 7 (right); © Tom W. Parkin, 8, 32
(left); © John Eastcott/Yva Momatiuk, 11;
© Francis Lepine, 17; © Val & Alan Wilkinson,
19; © Stephen Krasemann, 23 (right); © J. R.
Page, 29 (right); © Kennon Cooke, 31 (right);
© R. Moller, 40
© Map art by John Forsberg—4
COVER: Flooded Newport, Arkansas

Project Editor: Fran Dyra
Design: Margrit Fiddle

Library of Congress Cataloging-in-Publication Data

Erlbach, Arlene.
    Floods / by Arlene Erlbach.
        p.   cm.—(A New true book)
    Includes index.
    ISBN 0-516-01067-0
    1.   Floods—Juvenile literature. [1.   Floods.]
I.   Title.
GB1399.E75   1994
551.48'.9—dc20
                                                    94-14394
                                                    CIP
                                                    AC

WATER EVERYWHERE

Water covers 70 percent of the Earth's surface. It fills all our rivers, lakes, and oceans.

Sometimes rivers overflow their banks. Sometimes ocean waves roll onto land. When water flows over places that are normally dry, it causes a flood. Floods are common and natural occurrences. They happen all over the world.

Flooded farmland in Ontario, Canada

FLOODPLAINS

Areas of land along rivers are called floodplains. Many people like to live on or near floodplains. Many farms have been located close to rivers because floods

6

can bring valuable minerals to the soil. These minerals help crops grow.

Riverboats and barges provide transportation for people and goods. This is why many towns and cities have been built on rivers.

Barge traffic on the Mississippi River at St. Louis (left) and boats on the River Thames, London, England (right)

People use rivers for boating and swimming.

Some people live on rivers because they enjoy swimming, boating, and fishing. And houses built near water often have lovely settings and beautiful views.

Many floodplains flood regularly, and the floods usually cause little

Floodwaters covered the streets of Harpers Ferry, Virginia, in the spring of 1985.

damage. But some floods can be dangerous and destructive. Major floods can wash away buildings, houses, and cars. They can destroy crops. And people and animals may drown in floodwaters.

In the United States,

Cars and buses—and people—are often caught
in sudden floods from torrential rains.

floods kill more people
than any other weather-
related event. Floods
cause billions of dollars of
damage throughout the
world each year. Major
floods are one of the
world's most serious
natural disasters.

COASTAL FLOODS

When people hear about floods, they often think of rivers flooding. But areas near the ocean flood, too. This is called seacoast, or coastal, flooding.

High waves pushed up by hurricanes flood towns along the coasts.

Tsunami waves can flood shorelines very suddenly, causing death and destruction.

Sometimes coastal flooding is caused by a *tsunami*, or tidal wave. Tsunamis begin when an earthquake occurs on the ocean floor or when a seafloor volcano erupts.

The sudden jolt of the earthquake or eruption

disturbs the seafloor. That disturbance causes waves in the ocean. The waves travel outward from the source at speeds of up to 500 miles (805 kilometers) per hour.

In the open ocean, tsunami waves may be only 3 feet (1 meter) high. But when they reach shallow water near shore, the waves rise to 100 feet (30 meters) or more. Tsunamis cause massive flooding, destruction, and death.

HURRICANE GILBERT
SEPT. 15 1988
6 PM EDT

Hurricanes cause devastating winds and high waves.
Meteorologists track hurricanes to try to predict their
course. Satellite photos (inset) help them see the
shape and direction of the storm.

A hurricane may cause
coastal flooding, too.
Hurricanes are huge,
whirling rainstorms that
form over oceans and
travel toward land. The
winds in hurricanes reach

speeds as high as 150 miles (241 kilometers) per hour.

A hurricane's winds and rain push ocean waves up to 20 feet (6 meters) high. When these waves smash onto shore, the water flows across land for miles. This is called a storm surge. Most hurricane deaths occur in storm surges.

A hurricane's heavy rains deposit huge amounts of water on the land. This also causes coastal flooding.

RIVER FLOODS

River floods occur when a river or stream overflows. Rivers and streams are long, flowing, bodies of water that are usually lower than the land around them.

When rain falls, the ground soaks up some of the water. Trees and other plants absorb it through their roots. And some water seeps underground and becomes groundwater.

Floodwaters spread far and wide when the Richelieu River in Quebec, Canada, overflows.

But if too much rain falls, the soil becomes saturated. The ground cannot absorb all of it.

The extra water flows downhill into a river or stream and is carried to the ocean. But sometimes too much water flows into

17

a river or stream at one time. The river water rises higher and higher.

Finally, the river overflows its banks. Then the water floods onto the land.

Melting snow can cause floods, too. In the spring, the air warms. Heavy winter snows melt. But if the ground is still frozen, it cannot absorb water. The meltwater then flows into rivers and streams.

In spring, the meltwater from deep winter snows can cause a river to flood.

If too much melted snow flows into a river, the river rises over its banks. The height at which the river water begins to flow across the land is called the flood stage.

When a river is rising, people pile sandbags on the banks to try to hold back the water.

FLASH FLOODS

It usually takes several weeks of heavy rains for rivers to reach flood stage. People who live near such rivers can prepare for the flood and protect themselves.

But sometimes heavy rains cause a flash flood. Flash floods are sudden and extremely dangerous. Most flood deaths occur during flash floods.

Flash floods strike when rain falls in a torrential downpour. For example, cloudbursts from severe thunderstorms have caused many flash floods. The heavy rains of hurricanes can also cause flash floods.

During a severe rainstorm, water falls so fast that the ground cannot absorb it all. In a heavy downpour, an area may get as much rain in a few hours as it normally gets in a year.

Then, millions of gallons of water pour swiftly into rivers and streams. A tiny stream can quickly become a raging river.

Muddy water from a flash flood flows over a cliff that is normally dry (left). Small streams quickly become raging torrents during a flash flood (right).

The river cannot carry the water away fast enough. Soon, with little warning, rivers and streams overflow.

In 1976, a flash flood in Colorado caused 139

23

The Big Thompson River flood of 1976 washed out roads and swept away cars and buildings. At right, a rescue worker looks for victims in the floodwaters.

deaths and major destruction. The Big Thompson River overflowed after five hours of heavy rain. The downpour caused the usually shallow river to rise over 20 feet (6 meters).

HOW FLOODS DESTROY

Floodwaters are very powerful. They move fast. The water of a flash flood can travel at 20 miles (32 kilometers) per hour or more.

Once they hit land, tsunamis and storm surges cover people and property with frightening speed.

When a river floods, water pours into cities and towns. It gushes into buildings and houses.

Sometimes the worst part of flooding is the cleanup. The floodwater ruins furniture and other possessions. And when the water goes down, a layer of polluted mud covers floors and carpets.

The floodwater dumps sewage and mud into people's houses. Their furniture, appliances, and clothing are ruined.

Rushing waters can whisk away houses and

cars. The water's weight smashes everything in its path. The swift current carries everything along with it. Tree branches, windowpanes, and parts of buildings fly everywhere.

Most flood deaths occur when people are hit by objects swept along by the floodwater. Others die by drowning. Few people can swim against a floodwater's strong currents.

In the floods of 1993, the water treatment plant in Des Moines, Iowa, was put out of service. Trucks brought in clean water for drinking and cooking.

Although water is all around, floodwater is not safe to drink. It is dirty. It contains germs that make people sick. It pours into local water supplies and pollutes them.

A Mississippi River levee
near Burnside, Louisiana (left),
and a seawall at Vancouver,
British Columbia, Canada (right)

FLOOD BARRIERS

Nobody can control the weather that causes floods. So people try to hold water back. They build levees and dikes, flood walls and dams. These structures are called flood barriers.

Levees and dikes are

29

artificial riverbanks made of earth. They are built higher than the river itself so that the river can hold more water. Levees also narrow the river so that water flows faster.

High concrete flood walls are built along riverbanks. They keep water from flowing onto land.

Dams block rivers and streams and stop the flow of water. The water is held in a large lake, or reservoir, created in the

The water backed up by Hoover Dam (left)
in Nevada created Lake Mead (right).

river valley by the dam.
The reservoir water is
released when needed.

The Hoover Dam tames
the Colorado River. The
water held back creates
Lake Mead. Many people
use the lake for recreation. 31

Left: Water flows down from the reservoir to the power plant through pipes called penstocks. Right: The power plant at Hoover Dam

Water stored in a dam can be used to make electricity. First, the water is released through pipes called penstocks. Then the water flows over a wheel called a turbine.

weather stations check the flow of rivers. They use instruments called river gauges to predict water height. They use radar to predict rainfall.

Devices called flash flood alarms are attached to river piers. When the river water reaches a certain level, an alarm sounds. This alarm lets people know that a flash flood is about to occur.

At over sixty weather stations in the Pacific

Ocean, scientists study changes in the ocean floor. Certain changes warn that tsunamis may occur.

At the National Hurricane Center in Miami, Florida, meteorologists constantly watch for hurricanes. Satellites and radar help them predict hurricanes.

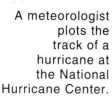
A meteorologist plots the track of a hurricane at the National Hurricane Center.

FLOOD WATCHES AND WARNINGS

TV stations, radio stations, and newspapers warn people about floods so that they can protect themselves.

Everyone should understand flood warnings and know what they mean. A *flood watch* means that a flood is possible. There is time to prepare for the flood. People should go to a safer area on higher ground.

A bus is caught in a flooded underpass.

A *flood warning* means that a flood will probably occur. People should lock up their houses and head for shelter in a safe area immediately.

During a flood it is important to follow safety rules:

Do not try to walk in

Sometimes floodwaters cover bridges and cut off roads.

floodwater. Do not swim in it.

Never drive over flooded areas. The floodwater may carry the car into deeper areas where it could overturn.

Do not go into a flooded area to see the damage. Do not return to get belongings once you have left.

Throw out any food touched by floodwater. Boil tap water before you use it.

It is important to heed flood warnings and take precautions. Many people have died in floods because they ignored warnings. They did not believe the flood would harm them.

In 1993 heavy rains brought floods to eight

The 1993 flood of the Mississippi River at Valmeyer, Illinois

states. The floods caused billions of dollars of damage but few deaths. Without our excellent warning systems, many people would have died.

THE WORLD'S WORST FLOODS

YEAR	PLACE	CAUSE	DEATHS
1824	Russia	River flood	10,000
1876	Bakarganj, India	Cyclone	200,000
1881	India	Cyclone	100,000
1881	Indochina	Typhoon	300,000
1883	Java and Sumatra	Tsunami	36,000
1887	Honan, China	Huang He River overflowed	900,000
1896	Japan	Tsunami	27,000
1931	China	River flood	145,000
1938	North China	Chinese blew up dikes to impede Japanese invasion	1 million
1942	India	Cyclone	40,000
1963	Bangladesh	Cyclone	22,000
1970	Bangladesh	Cyclone	250,000
1987	The Netherlands	Sea storm	50,000

WORST FLOODS IN NORTH AMERICA

DATE	PLACE	CAUSE	DEATHS
1861	California	Sacramento River overflowed	700
1874	Western Massachusetts	Dam failure	144
1889	Johnstown, Pennsylvania	Dam failure	over 2,000
1900	Galveston, Texas	Hurricane	over 6,000
1913	Ohio and Indiana	Ohio River overflowed	732
1926	Mexico	Dam failure	100
1928	Santa Paula, California	Dam failure	450
1929	Canada and Newfoundland	Tidal wave	27
1935	Mexico	Actopan River overflowed	400
1935	Mexico	Flash flood	100
1947	Mexico	Cloudburst	40
1954	Canada	Hurricane	83
1958	Mexico	(not listed)	26
1959	Haiti	Heavy rains	40
1971	Canada	Prolonged rain	31
1972	South Dakota	Dam failure	242
1972	West Virginia	Dam failure	125
1972	Mexico	Cloudburst	30
1973	Mexico City, Mexico	Thunderstorm	37
1976	Colorado	Flash flood of the Big Thompson River	139

WORDS YOU SHOULD KNOW

absorb (ub • ZORB)—to soak up

artificial (ar • tih • FISH • il)—made by people; not natural

barrier (BAIR • ee • yer)—a block; an obstruction that keeps something from moving forward

cloudburst (CLOWD • berst)—a storm in which a large amount of rain falls in a short time

current (KER • int)—a flow of water in a certain direction

dam (DAM)—a structure built across a river to control the flow of water and provide power to make electricity

destructive (dih • STRUK • tiv)—likely to destroy or ruin

dike (DYKE)—a wall built to keep a sea or river from flooding over land

disaster (dih • ZASS • ter)—an event that causes great damage or suffering

disturbance (dih • STER • bince)—a sudden change

diversion (dih • VER • zjun)—used to change direction

divert (dih • VERT)—to turn aside; to change the direction of a movement

earthquake (ERTH • kwaik)—the shaking of the ground caused by movements of rocks deep within the earth

erupt (ih • RUPT)—to burst out; to break out

gauge (GAIJE)—an instrument used to measure the amount of something

germs (JERMZ)—harmful bacteria that cause disease

hurricane (HER • ih • kain)—a strong storm with heavy rain and very high winds

levee (LEH • vee)—a bank of earth built along a river to keep it from overflowing

meteorologist (me • tee • or • AHL • ah • jist)—a scientist who studies weather

minerals (MIN • rilz)—substances in the soil that plants need to grow and be healthy

penstocks (PEN • stox)–pipes in dams that release water for use in making electricity

pollute (puh • LOOT)–to make dirty or poisonous

precautions (prih • KAW • shunz)–measures taken ahead of time to avoid danger

predict (prih • DIKT)–to tell what will happen in the future

radar (RAY • dar)–a device that finds objects by bouncing radio waves off them

reroute (ree • ROWT)–to send in a different direction or to a different place

reservoir (reh • zih • VWAHR)–an artificial lake that holds water for drinking or to make electric power

satellites (SAT • ill • ites)–a body, such as a moon, that revolves around a planet

saturated (SAT • cher • ay • tid)–completely soaked; holding as much water as it can

sewage (SOO • widj)–wastewater from houses and factories

storm surge (STORM SERJ)–a huge wave of water that comes onto land during a hurricane

torrential (tor • REN • shill)–overwhelming; like a torrent

tsunami (soo • NAH • mee)–a very high wave that comes onshore after an undersea earthquake or volcanic eruption

turbine (TER • byne)–an engine that is made to turn by the pressure of water or gas

valuable (VAL • yoo • ah • bil)–having great value; precious

volcano (vawl • KAY • no)–an opening in the Earth's crust through which material from inside the Earth erupts

INDEX

About the Author

Arlene Erlbach has written more than a dozen books for young people in many genres including fiction and nonfiction.

She has a master's degree in special education. In addition to being an author of children's books, she is a learning disabilities teacher at Gray School in Chicago, Illinois. Arlene loves to encourage children to write and is in charge of her school's Young Authors program.